John C. Thomas Jr.

T5-AGX-173

The University of Iowa took its roots from the people themselves.
From the outset, the Iowa pioneers had given evidence of their
devotion to education by the establishment of schools and academies.
This act of the first General Assembly was evidence of the people's
determination to have an institution of higher learning.

From *The Palimpsest*

Old Capitol

Law Building

The University of
Iowa

PHOTOGRAPHED BY JIM RICHARDSON

HARMONY HOUSE PUBLISHERS-LOUISVILLE

Executive Editors: William Butler and William Strode
Library of Congress Catalog Number: 87-083168
Hardcover International Standard Book Number 0-916509-32-X
Printed in Louisville, Kentucky by Fetter Printing Company
First Edition printed Fall, 1989 by Harmony House Publishers,
P.O. Box 90, Prospect, Kentucky 40059 (502) 228-2010 / 228-4446
Copyright © 1989 by Harmony House Publishers
Photographs Copyright © 1989 by Jim Richardson

This book or portions thereof may not be reproduced in any form without
permission of Harmony House Publishers. Photographs may not be
reproduced in any form without permission of Jim Richardson.

Danforth Chapel

INTRODUCTION

The University of Iowa. It is impossible to capture the spirit and the meaning behind that name with words alone. For each of the thousands of alumni who has walked beside the Iowa River, rushed to class on the Pentacrest to puzzle over a problematic essay exam, waved the black and gold banner on Saturday afternoon, or cheered the sublime artistry that performers have brought to Iowa's stages and concert halls, the University of Iowa means something unique.

If there is one symbol of this place that straddles the Iowa River, framed by the rolling cornfields in America's heartland, it must be the Old Capitol. A living museum used primarily for ceremonial purposes today, this edifice holds an important place in territorial, state, and university history.

But the Old Capitol alone is not definitive of the Iowa experience. The university's architecture is eclectic, representing the grace of what is old and the vigor of what is new. Macbride Hall, University Hospitals and Clinics, Hancher Auditorium, the Iowa Memorial Union, Schaeffer Hall, the Field House, Carver-Hawkeye Arena, the Engineering Building, Phillips Hall — all these places, too, represent the University of Iowa. Lessons have been learned in these buildings, friendships made, and memories stored.

For the moods of Iowa are many. Changeable as the seasons.

Macbride Hall

16

Colorful, calm, serendipitous. Intense. Serious. Sometimes frenzied. There is a spirit about Iowa that belies a simple description.

Perhaps more than anything, Iowa represents a community of people in quest for more — more wisdom, better understanding, the right answer, the reason for being, a solution to a problem that matters, not just for us, but for those who follow.

Since its founding in 1847, the University of Iowa has become a major intellectual and cultural center in the state, bringing together undergraduate, graduate, and professional students in a closely knit intellectual community with distinguished teachers and scholars. Studies spill beyond the classroom and into fervent discussion at some of Iowa City's favorite establishments.

The University of Iowa is no cloistered institution, but boasts a proud history of social involvement. Iowa was the first public university in the nation to admit men and women on an equal basis and the first institution of higher education to accept creative work in theater, writing, music, and art to fulfill thesis requirements for advanced degrees. The School of Religion was founded unapologetically to foster the study of religion, not to proselytize.

In every department and college, the University of Iowa embraces the world. Its research — whether it be directed to groundwater quality or the effectiveness of television advertising, to application of the death penalty or funding for education — affects public policy.

Iowa faculty developed and continue to hold preeminence in educational testing. Educational television began at Iowa, speech pathology was born here, and the university is known around the world for its distinguished writing programs.

In the highly competitive realm of science and technology, Iowa is relevant and renowned. Buffered aspirin was invented here; blood storage techniques responsible for saving so many lives were developed at Iowa; this university has been a pioneer in unmanned space research for 40 years; and scientists from around the world have been coming to Iowa to study hydraulic engineering even longer than that.

Today, Iowa remembers her past, but looks to a future that will depend on further advances in medicine, laser research, biomedical engineering, and environmental studies. It is a future that will demand the humanizing influence of the arts and the sense of community that allows for diversity and encourages daring inquiry.

The University of Iowa is a unique mix of people, places, and ideas. Somehow it works. Business majors rub shoulders with dancers, engineers discuss ethics, pharmacologists applaud the opera. Iowa has nurtured the writing talent of people like Flannery O'Connor, John Irving, and Paul Engle. It has given James Van Allen the opportunity for great explorations in space. Iowa is the place where Grant Wood taught painting and Arthur Steindler mended limbs. It is the home of the beloved Hawkeyes.

There is no place like the University of Iowa. No place in the world. And, even if the place could be duplicated, the people who have made Iowa so special cannot.

University President Hunter Rawlings, not an Iowan himself, has observed that Iowans are taproot people with values that run deep and memories that run long. We suspect that he is right. And we hope that this book, with photographs both old and new, will rekindle for you your own memories of the University of Iowa.

A Selected University Chronology

1840	Old Capitol (ownership transferred to the university in 1857)
1855-59	President Amos Dean
1859-62	President Silas Totten
1862-67	President Oliver M. Spencer
1867-68	Acting President Nathan Ransom Leonard
1868-70	President James Black
1870-71	Acting President Nathan Ransom Leonard
1871-77	President George Thacher
1877-78	Acting President Christian W. Slagle
1878-87	President Josiah Little Pickard
1884	Calvin Hall (moved to its present location in 1905)
1887-98	President Charles Ashmead Schaeffer
1897	Seashore Hall (formerly University Hospital, later named East Hall)
1898-99	Acting President Amos Noyes Currier
1899-1911	President George Edwin MacLean
1902	Schaeffer Hall (formerly Collegiate Hall)
1905	Engineering Building
1908	Macbride Hall (formerly Hall of Natural Science)
1910	Gilmore Hall (formerly North Hall, first Law Building)
1911-14	President John Gabbert Bowman
1912	President's Home, MacLean Hall
1913	Currier Hall
1914-16	President Thomas Huston Macbride
1916-34	President Walter Albert Jessup
1919	Steindler Building (formerly Children's Hospital)
1920	Quadrangle
1924	Iowa Memorial Union
1926	Jessup Hall (formerly University Hall)
1927	Field House
1928	General Hospital
1929	Kinnick Stadium (formerly Iowa Stadium)
1934-40	President Eugene Allen Gilmore
1936	Theatre Building
1940	Acting President Chester Arthur Phillips
1940-64	President Virgil Melvin Hancher
1951	Main Library
1954	Hospital School
1958	Burge Hall
1963	Pharmacy Building
1964-69	President Howard Rothmann Bowen
1965	Van Allen Hall (formerly Physics Building), Phillips Hall
1966	Nursing Building
1968	Wendall Johnson Speech and Hearing Center
1969-81	President Willard Lee Boyd, Jr.
1969	Museum of Art
1971	Music Building
1972	Hancher Auditorium
1973	Dental Science Building
1976	Alumni Center
1981-82	Acting President Duane C. Spriestersbach
1982	Communications Center
1982-87	President James O. Freedman
1987-88	Acting President Richard D. Remington
1988	President Hunter R. Rawlings III
1984	Carver-Hawkeye Arena
1985	Boyd Law Building
1991	Laser Facility

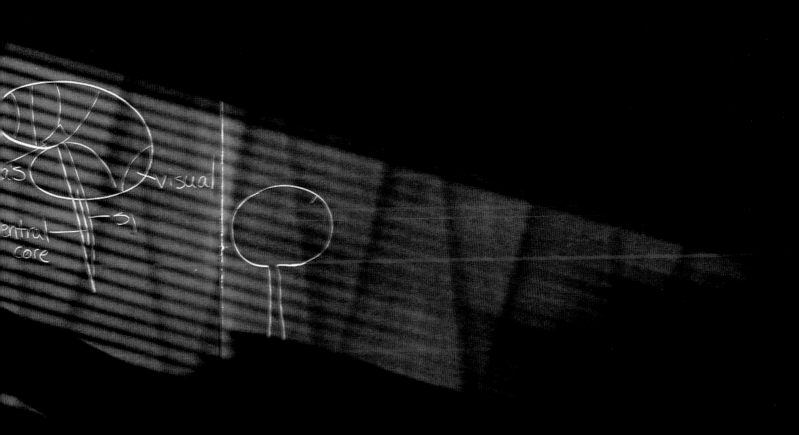

Having obtained the teachers, we must have buildings and equipment, and the more commodious the buildings and complete the apparatus, the greater the advantage both to teacher and pupil. But as the body without the soul, so are the material adjuncts of a University without able and zealous professors. And as a great mind may inhabit a poor body and yet influence the world, so may the best instruction be given in modest quarters.

President Charles Schaeffer, inaugural address, June, 1887

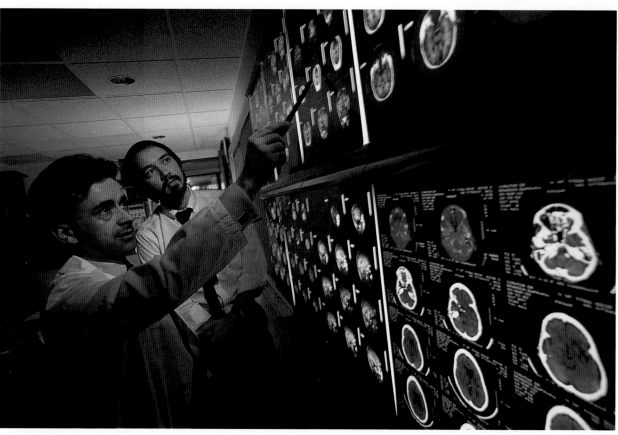

College of Medicine

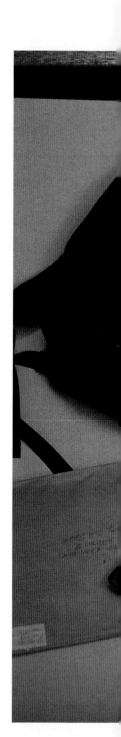

College of Business Administration

And here the question arises. What is a university, or rather, what ought it to be? It is not only an institution where knowledge is disseminated, but where it is also originated. It is a place both for instruction and investigation...

President Silas Totten, 1860

Boyd Tower

A window and a river. Butterflies
Lazily flapping through August's heavy air.
Incessant shrill of crickets: the great oak
Looming over your balcony: the moon
Impossibly bright above the Iowa River.
Akhudiat dancing, sinuous as the river.
"Flesh, heaven, angels, poetry and bestsellers!"
How humdrum life seems elsewhere; for a time
An ideal world is almost realized
Through writers meeting, talking, arguing,
Translating, drinking, even writing, while
The crickets lapse to silence and the oak
Starts dropping acorns and the moon chills
And the snow begins to fall on Iowa.

Iowa Recollected in Tranquility, Peter Jay
from *The World Comes to Iowa*

29

30   *University of Iowa Hospitals and Clinics*

College of Dentistry

34   *Old Capitol*

Halsey Gymnasium

Greek Follies

Sorority Candle Passing

O, Iowa, calm and secure on thy hill
Looking down on the river below,
With a dignity born of the dominant will
Of the men that lived long ago,
O, heir of the glory of pioneer days,
Let thy spirit be proud as of old,
For thou shalt find blessing and honor and praise
In the daughters and sons of Old Gold.

We shall sing and be glad with the days as they fly
In the time that we spend in thy halls,
And in the sadness we'll part when the days have gone by
And the path turns away from thy walls.
Till the waters no more in thy river shall run
Till the stars in the heavens grow cold
We shall sing of the glory and fame thou hast won
And the love that we bear for Old Gold.

The Old Gold Hymn, John C. Parrish, 1905

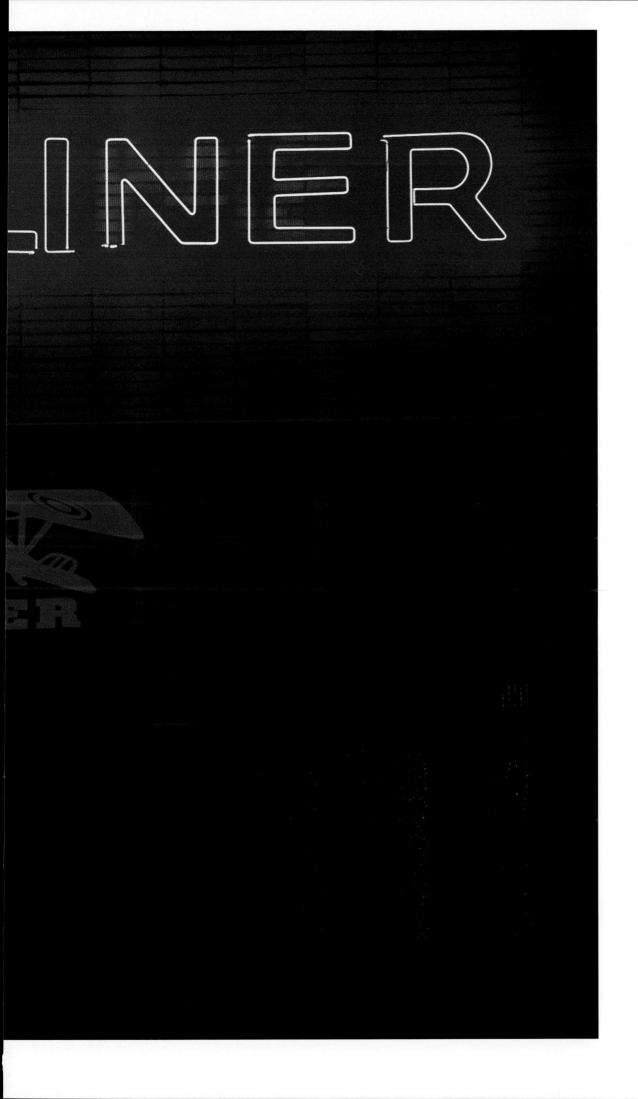

Iowa City is a small town with lots of squirrels skipping about the lawns and sidewalks, climbing the fir trees, the cedars, and the maples. The squirrels outnumber the 60,000 inhabitants, half of whom are students from all over the U.S. and foreign countries. These young nomads, dressed in the Hawkeye football team's black and yellow, stroll down the main streets from classroom to classroom, library to cafeteria, crowding the fraternities and sororities. The town's residents live in the security of their tranquil green and idyllic streets. The wooden houses form enviable rows of eye-catching styles, Colonial, Georgian, and Victorian; each house differs from the houses next door. This variety of porches, pillars, roofs, and embellishments still forms a harmonious whole. There are no fences to separate the houses from each other or from the streets, nor are the doors locked, so the story goes.

Aharon Megged, from *The World Comes to Iowa*

Downtown Walking Mall

45

Iowa River Bridge

The Coralville Reservoir

Those days of autumn, when the river would turn bloody red — and then into a gentle glimmer of gold, the shifting tints on the leaves, blinking lights of the dorms — no, they haven't yet congealed into a memory. They are still too near and palpable for me to acquire the dim remoteness of a memory. Later, perhaps, I will remember them with a certain sense of equanimity and detachment, but at the moment, they only bring a sharp pang of separation.

Nirmal Verma, from *The World Comes to Iowa*

Bowen Science Building

Preceding page: Medical Research Center

When I talk about my stay in Iowa to a great many
Americans (and in particular to New Yorkers) they
always grin at first as if I were talking about a Godfor-
saken place of no character or something accidental. But
I stauchly insist that if foreigners (and maybe even
Americans) want to understand America from within, to
comprehend the seeds of its identity, places like Iowa City
are the places to begin.

There both halves of the kernel of American identity are
quite plain, with neither masks nor husks — American
liberalism, individualism, kindheartedness and warmth,
as well as the stubborn, almost wild, conservatism that
together constitute the essence of America.

A.B. Yehoshua, from *The World Comes to Iowa*

Communications Center

Hancher Auditorium

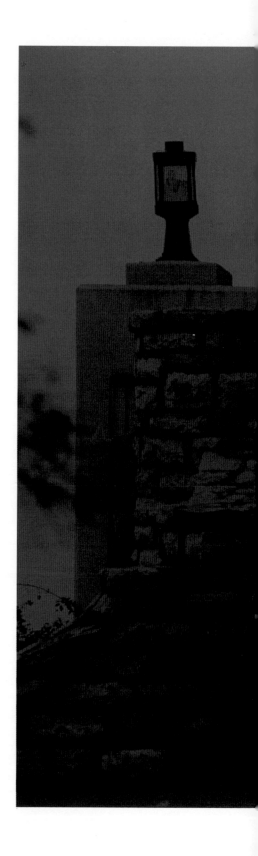

Union Footbridge

Special Collections — Iowa Cultural Memorabilia

It is deceptively easy to take the University of Iowa or any large institution for granted. To assume that the buildings and facilities we see and use, the classes we see listed in the schedule of courses, the academic and social mores by which the university guides us — and we it — have always been, and for all we know, always will be.

Not so. Everything has its past; more often than not, the larger and more complex the thing, the more expansive and involved is its history.

A university however, is not simply a thing. Its growth and the inevitable intricacies that accompany that growth have always, and always will, depend upon people.

Larry Perl, from *Calm and Secure on Thy Hill*

College of Pharmacy

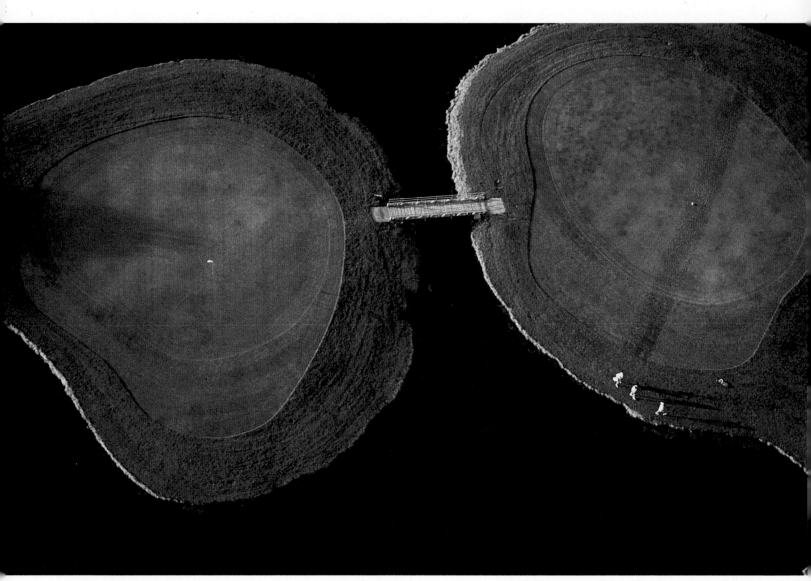

Finkbine Golf Course

Hawkeye Baseball Stadium

The word is "Fight! Fight! Fight! for Iowa,"
Let every loyal Iowan sing;
The word is "Fight! Fight! Fight! for Iowa,"
Until the walls and rafters ring (Rah! Rah!)
Come on and cheer, cheer, cheer, for Iowa
Come on and cheer until you hear the final gun.
The word is "Fight! Fight! Fight! for Iowa,"
Until the game is won.

The Iowa Fight Song, Meredith Willson

Carver-Hawkeye Arena

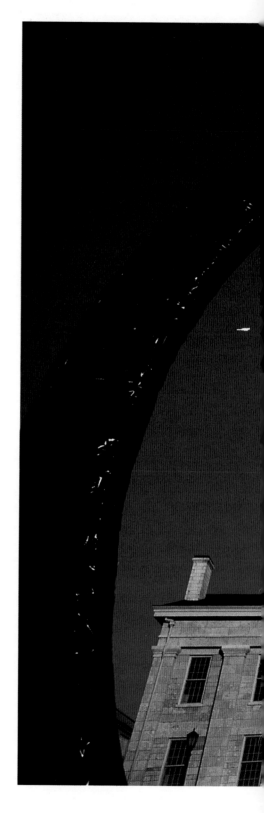

Leaves are starting to change color, the nights are getting cooler, and the stifling heat of the summer is mostly an unpleasant memory.

Fall has come to Iowa City and to the University of Iowa campus, and once again, as it has been throughout the 1980s, Saturdays are Fry-days, and the campus, the city, and the state are alive with excitement.

Al Grady '49 in *Alumni Review*, September, 1987

The Corn Monument

Kinnick Stadium

There's a War in Europe, But Right Now —
HAWKEYES TAKE INDIANA, 32-29

Headline from the *Daily Iowan*, October 8, 1939

75

Floyd of Rosedale

The Pentacrest

This early statehouse remains Iowa's most precious material monument — the birthplace of statehood, honored by the presence of the founders of territory and state, by the addresses from the very spot by the war Governor ... and consecrated by the professors and young patriots who have gone forth from its halls. Plain, solid, symmetrical, it stands for Iowa, and shall ever be the heart of the University.

George E. MacLean, President, 1899-1911

Macbride Hall

Museum of Art Patio

Schaeffer Hall

If I were to epitomize my hopes for this second century, they would pass beyond great structures in marble or brick or stone, or gigantic libraries or vast and impressive laboratories — useful and necessary as these may be. My hopes would center around a changing emphasis, a changing point of view concerning education and the educational process... it is my hope that we may achieve a more complete understanding of the fact that education is a lifelong process, that it continues from birth to death, that the university is not concerned alone with the brief span of years—from two, four, six, or eight — spent upon this campus but with the years beyond and with the capacity of its alumni to grow in wisdom and in stature adequate for the complex, exacting, yet fascinating civilization which will unfold in the University's second century.

President Virgil Hancher, Founder's Day Address, February, 1948

One of the happy results of such a bursting of activities in the arts was that Iowa citizens could stun most New Yorkers by remarking — with studied casualness, of course — that they had had dinner with Horowitz, enjoyed a poolside buffet with Seiji Ozawa, and shared an outdoor picnic with the Joffrey dancers, not to mention entertaining such writers as John Cheever and Anthony Burgess on many occasions.

John C. Gerber from *A Pictorial History of the University of Iowa*

Museum of Art

85

The University of Iowa has long had to rely on originality of ideas, creative imagination, and new concepts. It was surely the first institution to state in its catalog that a thesis for an advanced degree could be a contribution to knowledge or a book of poems or fiction, a play (when working on his plays in Iowa City, Tennessee Williams served food behind the counter in the Memorial Union cafeteria), a musical composition, a painting, a sculpture, or a dance. The result was that in all areas of the arts there was not only historical instruction, but also an emphasis on creating a new work.

From *The World Comes to Iowa* — Introduction
by Hualing Nieh Engle and Paul Engle

Scottish Highlanders

Art Building

In this pleasant valley the people of the Commonwealth of Iowa have generously provided you with a great university. Here there has been collected a community of scholars and teachers who will guide you in the fields. They will be a stimulus and an inspiration to you.

President Virgil Hancher, September, 1940, his final address to incoming freshmen

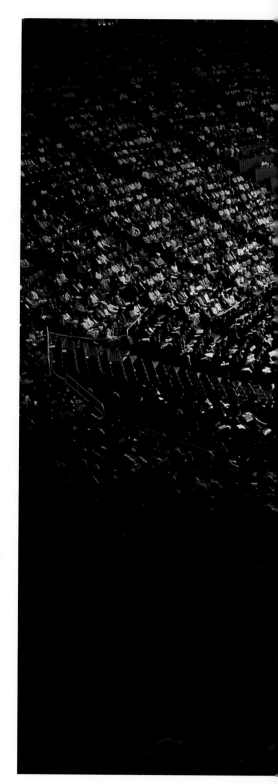

Commencement: Carver-Hawkeye Arena

On, Iowa, on forevermore,
On, Iowa, proudly at the fore
Ev'ry loyal son will give a rousing toast to you,
Ev'ry loyal daughter loves you true,
On, Iowa, with your wealth untold,
A heritage to us you did unfold,
Love of family, love of friend,
Love of country, too, makes us proud for what you stand
Our dear Old Gold.

On Iowa by W.R. Law '04

Restored House Chamber, Old Capitol

UNIVERSITY OF IOWA
Pictures From the Past

Old Capitol and South Hall shown in an engraving, ca. 1862

How did it come to be? Our beginnings were so shaky, the baby so weak and frail at birth that for a while it looked as though Iowa would never make it. Rome, however, as some old codger remembered, was not built in a day. And Iowa's traditions of high falutin supremacy are all the more serious because it took years of struggle, patience and suffering to get us to the place where we are.

Nicholas Meyer, in the introduction to *Calm and Secure on Thy Hill*, by Larry Perl

Left to right, South Hall, Old Capitol
and North Hall, ca. 1880. The fence in
the foreground kept roving livestock
off the campus lawns

Calvin Hall in the 1890s. To the left through the trees can be seen the North Hall Observatory

The Medical Building, South College, Old Capitol, North Hall and the Dental Science Building ca. 1895

The Fieldhouse, 1927

Mechanic's Academy — site of the first classrooms of the University. It was built in 1842 and stood on the site of East Hall

View from west of Iowa Avenue bridge, 1925

Ice skating on the Iowa River, 1890

Burlington Street bridge and dam, with the campus in the background, ca. 1925

View from east of the river, ca. 1895. From left to right are Old Dental, North Hall, Old Capitol, South Hall, Old Medical

Pentacrest sidewalk, looking east toward Iowa Avenue in 1915

Iowa Avenue looking east from Old Capitol, November, 1927

The Law Library in Old Capitol, ca. 1900. This library was situated in the old Senate chamber

A women's physical education class inside Halsey Gymnasium, 1927

A crowd convenes on the Pentacrest for a University function, 1890s

College of Dentistry students and their patients gather for a group photograph in the 1930s

The Hawkeye football team, 1898

Alex Karras, two-time All American, winner of the
Outland Trophy in 1958, and "Lineman of the Year "

Alex Karras and Mac Lewis rush Notre Dame quarterback Bob Williams
in the last game of the 1958 season. Iowa won this game 21-13, and
finished the season at 7-1-1

Iowa wins the Rose Bowl with a 38-12 win over Cal in 1959 under coach
Forest Evashevski. The team ends the season 8-1-1

1956, the senior year of the Fabulous Five — Schoof, Logan, Cain, Seaberg and Scheuerman. The Hawkeyes win the Big Ten two years in a row, but lose to Bill Russell-led San Francisco in the NCAA finals, 83-71

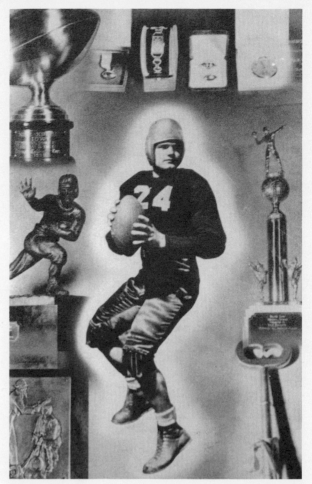

After the 1955 Hawkeyes defeated Minnesota 72-70 to win the Big Ten, 2000 students mobbed the plane bringing the team home the next day

Heisman Trophy winner Nile Kinnick, hailed as the greatest football player Iowa has ever produced

This rough and ready bunch looks like an athletic team, but in fact it is the Class of 1907

Robert Frost and Paul Engle at the famous Iowa Writers Workshop

President Virgil Hancher spoke at the Navy Preflight School inauguration ceremonies in April, 1942

Famous Iowans Grant Wood (top) and Thomas Hart Benton wear false mustaches and beards in this gag photograph from 1935. They were members of the SPCS Club — the Society for the Prevention of Cruelty to Speakers

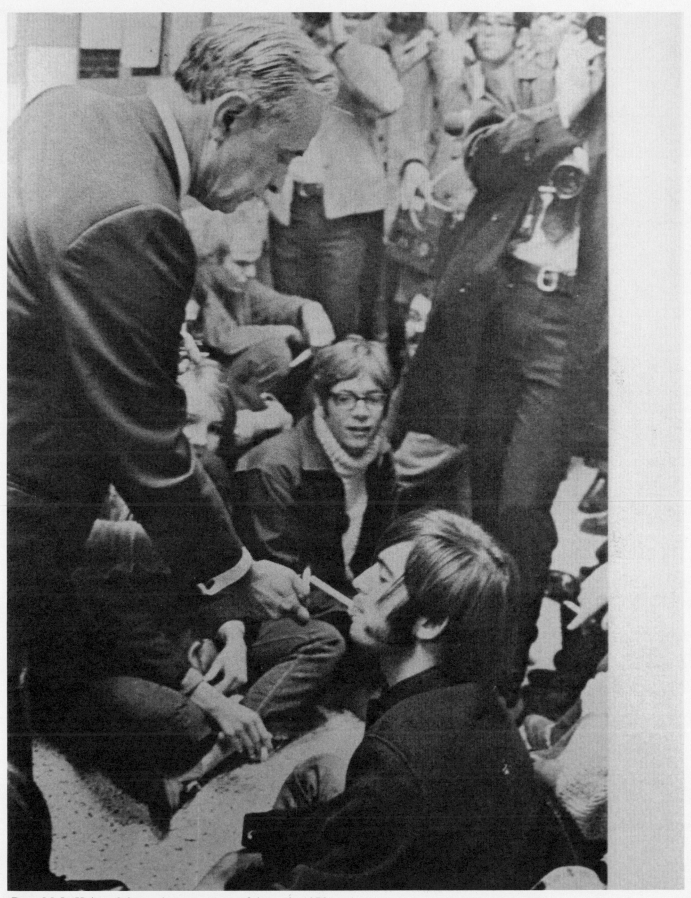

Dean M. L. Huit and the student protestors of the early 1970s

Mountain to mountain rich fields roll,
ocean of soil above an ocean of stone,
limestone beds that were once a seabed,
full of hard fossils, making sweet dirt.
Feeding far countries that have never seen it,
this land rolls onward with the rolling world,
a place of trust in a time not to be trusted.

Excerpt from *Heartland*, by Paul Engle